KW-221-888

Contents

Nan
and the
Baaad
Sheep

Cas Lester

Illustrated by
Freya Hartas

OXFORD

OXFORD

UNIVERSITY PRESS

Great Clarendon Street, Oxford, OX2 6DP,
United Kingdom

Oxford University Press is a department of the University of Oxford.
It furthers the University's objective of excellence in research, scholarship,
and education by publishing worldwide. Oxford is a registered trade mark of
Oxford University Press in the UK and in certain other countries

Text © Cas Lester 2017

Illustrations © Freya Hartas 2017

The moral rights of the author have been asserted

First published 2017

British Library Cataloguing in Publication Data
Data available

978-0-19-837768-9

3 5 7 9 10 8 6 4 2

Paper used in the production of this book is a natural, recyclable product
made from wood grown in sustainable forests. The manufacturing process
conforms to the environmental regulations of the country of origin.

Printed in China by Leo Paper Products Ltd.

Acknowledgements
Inside cover notes written by Gill Howell
Author photograph by Isabella Valentine

For Nan,

who was a wonderful gran

Chapter 1
Baaad Sheep!

Monday

It was a boiling hot day on the farm. Nan, the farmer, was building a sheep pen in the corner of the field. "Walloping wool bags! It's far too hot to be doing this," she puffed, as she dragged a heavy metal gate across the grass. She was sweltering in her blue overalls and rubber welly boots.

"It's a lot cooler under here!" grinned Nelly the sheepdog. She was lying beneath the tractor in the shade, with her grey muzzle resting on her paws.

Now, I don't want you thinking that Nelly was being lazy. She wasn't. It's just that dogs can't build sheep pens. They don't have hands and they can't lift.

On the other side of the field, the sheep stood watching Nan uneasily.

"Hey, Old Smelly, what's going on?" one of them called out to Nelly, rudely. This particular sheep had a pink plastic ear tag with the number 38 printed on it.

"Nan's building you a pen because it's time to get you all in for shearing," answered Nelly. "And you know how much you love being turned upside-down and having all your wool shaved off," she laughed.

"Nooo!" wailed the horrified sheep. They hated being sheared.

"Bad luck! Or should I say, 'Baaad luck'?" gloated Nelly. "And don't call me 'Old Smelly'!" she added crossly.

"Why not? You're old and you stink baaadly," replied Pink 38 cheekily.

"I'm not old. I'm only twelve," retorted Nelly. "And I don't stink!"

Actually, twelve is *quite* old for a sheepdog. But then, Nan is seventy-three! And that's *very* old for a sheep farmer. In fact, she's old enough to be your grandma, or even your great-grandma.

But anyhow, by now Nan had finished making the pen so she whistled loudly to Nelly. "Come on, old girl. Let's get these silly girls rounded up and into the pen before we all melt."

And that's when the fun and games began.

Nan and Nelly have been rounding sheep up for years and are pretty good at it. The problem is the sheep are even better at *not* being rounded up.

"Baa-baa-ba-ba-ba! Can't catch me-ee!" they laughed, and scattered across the field.

"Oh, don't start mucking about, you silly old woolly sacks!" yelled Nan crossly, chasing after them. "Why can't

you just get in the pen? You know that's
what I want you to do!"

Nan charged around one side of the sheep, and Nelly shot off around the other. She was aiming for Pink 38 – who was always the troublemaker.

"There's no point giving me the run-around. You'll have to come into the pen sooner or later," Nelly told Pink 38.

"You'll have to catch me first!" Pink 38 laughed, and suddenly darted off to one side.

"Oh, for crying out loud," panted Nelly, following her. "You'll be much cooler without all that manky old wool."

"But it's so uncomfortable being sheared," complained Pink 38.

"How would you like to have all your fur shaved off?" agreed her friend, Yellow 14.

"Now you're being ridiculous," puffed Nelly.

On the other side of the field, Nan was doing her best to herd some of the other sheep into the pen. But they were running rings around her.

"It's fun being baaad!" they laughed.

"Shambling sheepdogs!" cried Nan. "Why are you always so naughty?"

Nan's poor old knees were a bit dodgy and she couldn't run fast any more. And to make it even worse, the sheep kept changing direction.

Dart ... swerve ... twist ... "Baa-ha-ha-ha!" They thought it was hilarious!

"I am not finding this funny!" cried Nan. "I'm too hot and I'm too old and my knees are too creaky for this lark."

Finally, Nan managed to get a few of the sheep into the pen. But before she could swing the metal gate shut behind them, they turned and ran straight back out again – and knocked her over!

"Shuddering shepherds!" she wailed, landing smack in a dollop of mud.

SPLAT!

"Right! THAT'S IT!" she bellowed, scrambling to her feet. "Nelly!"

The sheepdog ran over to her, panting hard and with her tongue lolling out. Nan ruffled the fur between Nelly's ears. "Come on, old girl. We're going home. We'll try again tomorrow." Nan clambered on to the tractor. Nelly scrabbled up beside her and Nan drove off.

The sheep didn't stop laughing for hours.

Chapter 2
Break Out!

Tuesday

The next day, Nan was up and about in the farmyard bright and early.

"Nelly old girl, I have had a rather brilliant idea," she told the sheepdog.

Nelly raised one doggy eyebrow and looked at her.

"Those greedy sheep will do anything for food," said Nan. "So I'm going to put a trough in the pen and fill it with sheep food. They'll come racing in then," she laughed. "And we won't even have to round them up at all."

"Ha! An excellent plan!" thought Nelly, grinning and wagging her tail. "That'll show those stroppy sheep who's boss!"

Nan shoved a couple of feeding troughs into the back of the trailer. She chucked in a few sacks of sheep food, too.

Grabbing the steering wheel, she pulled herself up into the driving seat of the tractor. Nelly jumped up beside her. Then the tractor trundled along the narrow road to the field, with the trailer rattling along noisily behind it.

CREAK! CLANK!

"Come on, old Rusty Guts!" cried
Nan as the old tractor chugged its way
slowly up the narrow lane. "You can
do it."

Nan's tractor wasn't just old – it was
ancient. In fact, it was probably even
older than Nan. And that says a lot! It
was more rust than metal, with a lot of
mud holding everything together.

RATTLE! RATTLE! CHUG!

"Keep going, Rusty Guts!" Nan cried.
The ancient tractor finally managed to
clatter up the lane, but when they got to
the field ... the sheep weren't there!

"Wobbling woolly jumpers!"
exclaimed Nan. "Where are they?"

The sheep had escaped from the field!
They were running all over the road,
baaing and bleating and laughing their
heads off. They thought it was hilarious.

"You are the naughtiest sheep I have
ever had in fifty years!" cried Nan.

Nelly leaped off the tractor and rushed up to the sheep. "What do you think you're playing at?" she barked angrily.

"We're having a day out," announced Pink 38 mischievously.

"We thought we'd pop into the village," Yellow 14 added.

"Get back in that field!" snapped Nelly.

"Can't make me," replied Pink 38 cheekily, and she shot off down the lane towards the village. "Baa-baa-ba-ba-ba! Can't catch me-ee!" she laughed.

The rest of the flock bolted after her, rudely waggling their woolly tails behind them.

"Nelly, get in front of them!" yelled Nan. "We've got to stop them!"

Nelly tried, but the lane was too narrow and she couldn't get past the sheep to overtake them. "Move over," she woofed.

"Shaaan't!" they baaed.

"Oh, for crying out loud," snapped Nelly. "This is ridiculous."

"Yes, but isn't it fun?" bleated Pink 38.

"No, it's not!" retorted Nelly.

"Fluttering fleeces!" groaned Nan. "It'll be chaos if they get into the village. They'll hold up all the traffic and we'll never manage to catch them."

But the sheep simply refused to let Nelly get past. There was nothing she could do but chase after them.

"Oh, good grief," thought Nelly. "This is so embarrassing."

"Baaa-ha-ha-ha!" laughed Pink 38 over her shoulder. "You're getting too old for this, Old Smelly."

"Don't be so cheeky," retorted the sheepdog.

Furiously, Nan left the tractor in a gateway and chased after the flock on foot. In front of her, the entire lane was a sea of waddling sheep. "Walloping welly boots! Come back here, you daft great woolly-brained beasties," she bawled.

Chapter 3
Chaos in the Village

The sheep clattered down into the
village, bleating excitedly – and
completely blocked the main road.
There was an angry BEEP BEEEEEEP
and a SCREECH of brakes.

"Mind the bus!" yelled Nan, as
the sheep hurtled towards it. The bus
skidded to a stop, surrounded by sheep.

"Road hog!" huffed Pink 38.

"Dangerous driver!" bleated Yellow 14.

"Get those sheep off the road!" yelled the bus driver to Nan.

"That's what I'm trying to do," she cried.

The sheep had spied an open gate. The driver and all the passengers clambered off the bus to help Nan.

"Don't you dare go into that garden!" warned Nelly.

"Roses!"

"Lilies!"

"Daisies!"

"Marigolds!"

The sheep charged into the garden and promptly starting munching everything in sight.

"Get those sheep out of my flowers!" yelled the owner of the garden, bursting out of his front door.

"I'm working on it," panted Nan, rushing up with Nelly and herding the sheep back through the gate.

But the sheep headed straight for the village shop!

"Oh, for crying out loud," barked Nelly. "Now you're just being stupid!"

"Shuffling shepherds! NOOOO!" wailed Nan.

But the sheep had seen what was inside the shop.

"Apples!"

"Carrots!"

"Cabbages!"

"Cauliflowers!"

They stormed in through the door, barging each other out of the way.

"Shoo, shoo!" cried the shopkeeper, herding them back out again with a broom. "Get these sheep under control," she shouted at Nan.

"I wish I could," puffed poor old Nan.

Suddenly, there was an ear-piercing siren and a police car pulled up.

"Uh-oh!" groaned Nan.

A police officer got out and waded through the sheep towards Nan.

"Excuse me, madam, are these your sheep?" she asked. "They can't just run wild in the village. You'll have to catch them."

"That's what I'm trying to do!" spluttered Nan. So the police officer, the bus driver, the passengers, Nelly and Nan all tried to round up the mischievous sheep. But the flock gave them the slip and ran off up the road – and into the school!

It was sports day and everyone was on the playing field. The sheep charged across the running track and into the middle of a race! They shot past the racing children, towards the finishing line. Pink 38 won, with Yellow 14 coming second and Nelly a close third.

"Baaad luck, Old Smelly," Pink 38 gloated, doing a lap of honour around the playing field.

Nelly sank down on to the grass, exhausted. "This is the most humiliating day of my life," she groaned in despair. Nan thought so, too. The children, on the other hand, thought it was the best sports day *ever*.

Finally, with everyone's help, the sheep were rounded up. Then Nelly, Nan and the police officer herded them back along the lane and into the field.

"Waddling wool sacks! What a day," cried Nan in relief, as she slammed the gate shut behind them.

"Well, that was fun," laughed Pink 38.

"Yes, let's do it again," agreed Yellow 14.

"Oh, good grief," said Nelly, rolling her eyes.

"Hey! There's a whacking great hole in the fence," said the police officer. "No wonder the sheep got out. You need a new fence."

"No I don't," scoffed Nan, going over to have a look. "I can mend that."

Nelly guarded the gap in the fence so the sheep couldn't escape again. Meanwhile, Nan drove the tractor back to the farmyard to fetch her tools and a new bit of wire fence.

SMACK! WHACK! THWACK!

Nan nailed the new piece of fence to the wooden fence posts, and covered up

the hole. "Come on, Nelly. It's too late to get those sheep into their pen now. Are you ready for some supper?"

"What sort of question is that?" thought the sheepdog. "I'm always ready for supper!"

But as they drove back down the lane towards the farm, Rusty Guts suddenly began to make some very alarming noises.

Chapter 4
Breakdown!

GRUMBLE! GRIND! GROAN!

"Trundling tractors! I don't like the sound of that," announced Nan.

"Uh-oh!" thought Nelly. "That doesn't sound good."

"Do not break down, Rusty Guts! Please!" begged Nan.

But suddenly, there was a mighty BANG, BONK, RATTLE and KER-PLUNK! The tractor juddered to a stop.

"Festering foot rot!" bellowed Nan. She took out her phone and called one of her farmer friends, asking him to tow them home with his tractor.

"And can you please hurry?" she added. "I'm stuck right in the middle of the lane."

"Don't worry, I'm on my way," he told her.

Just then there was an angry BEEP
BEEEEEP and a SCREECH of brakes.

"Move over, you're blocking the
road!" yelled an angry voice. It was
the bus driver. Nan had managed to
hold her up for the second time
that day.

KERPLUNK!

"Oh no!" Nan cringed in
embarrassment.

By the time Nan's friend arrived, the
bus, a delivery truck and two cars were
stuck behind Rusty Guts.

"Can this day get any worse?" muttered Nan. Just at that moment, there was a rumble of thunder and a flash of lightning – and it started raining.

"Yes, it can," groaned Nelly, as the rain soaked into her fur.

Nan's farmer friend's tractor was enormous. It was also brand new and very expensive. "Go and sit in the cab, out of the rain," the farmer told Nan as he fixed the tow link on to Rusty Guts.

So Nan did, and Nelly was just about to follow when the farmer stopped her. "Oi! You're not getting in my lovely clean cab – you're all muddy!"

"She can sit on my lap," offered Nan.

"No chance!" said the farmer.

So poor old Nelly had to walk. "I am not having a good day," she thought, plodding home through the puddles.

"We were lucky to get that rusty old heap of a tractor back in one piece," said Nan's farmer friend when they got into the farmyard. "I thought it was going to fall to bits on the road!"

"It's not that bad," said Nan, giving the ancient tractor a kindly thump on the bonnet.

"Yes it is! You should give it to a museum," laughed her friend.

"Nonsense!" exclaimed Nan. "There's tons of life in the old thing yet. I can fix it."

"You won't be able to get any parts. It's far too old," said her friend.

When she got into the kitchen, Nan kicked off her muddy welly boots and peeled off her damp overalls. Then she put the heating on.

Nelly lay down next to the radiator. As the warmth started to dry her soggy fur, she steamed gently and the horrible smell of wet dog wafted up Nan's nose.

"Oh, yuk!" she cried. "You're a right 'Old Smelly' tonight, aren't you?" she joked.

"Oh, don't you start," thought Nelly.

Nan shoved a fish pie into the microwave to cook and then she fed Nelly. Nan ate her supper at the kitchen table in front of her laptop, while she searched the Internet looking for a new part for Rusty Guts.

But by bedtime she'd given up. "It's hopeless, old girl, I can't find one anywhere," she said. "Nobody makes new parts for old tractors any more. Shambling shepherds! What am I going to do now?"

"Good question," thought Nelly.

Chapter 5
Enough is Enough

Wednesday

The next morning, Nan fed Nelly her breakfast and then ate hers. "I need to fix the tractor," she said, slurping her coffee. "If I can't find a new part I'll just have to mend the old one."

Nan went to get her toolbox. Then she pulled the broken part off Rusty Guts and took it into her workshop.

Nan's workshop was in an old stable, and it was full of stuff she'd been collecting – for *fifty* years! She didn't throw things away in case they came in useful. So it was stuffed with boxes and bins, all overflowing with nuts and bolts, old tools, bits of broken tractor parts and odd bits of metal.

The broken part of the tractor had snapped in half, so Nan looked for something to mend it with. She rooted around and suddenly pounced on a small, flat piece of metal. "Aha! That'll be perfect," she cried.

Nan pulled on a pair of thick leather gloves and put her welding helmet over her face to protect her from flying sparks. Then she got out her welder, switched it on and lit the blowtorch. WHOOSH! The flame was blindingly bright and hot enough to melt metal. Sparks flew out like a firework going off as Nan welded the piece of metal on to the old tractor part.

Then she switched off the blowtorch, took off her helmet and inspected the mend carefully. "That's not bad at all," she said proudly. And when she put the mended part back on to the tractor, old Rusty Guts started up first time.

Nan poked her head around the kitchen door. Nelly was still in her bed.

"Come on, lazybones," she cried. "Let's go and get those sheep."

Nelly looked up but didn't get out of bed. Now, I don't want you to think Nelly was being lazy. She wasn't. She's never been late for work, or had a day off in her life. It's just that she wasn't feeling very well.

"Achoooo!" she sneezed. "ACHOOOOO!"

"What's up, old girl?" asked Nan. Despite her stiff knees, she knelt down next to Nelly.

Nelly sniffed, and thumped her tail.

"Hmmm. Your nose is dry, your eyes are runny and you keep ..."

"Achoooooo!" went Nelly.

" ... sneezing!" said Nan. "You've got a cold! Stay here and rest. I'll get those daft old sheep in by myself. I'll use my sneaky sheep food trick."

So Nan went up to the field on the tractor. It was a bit difficult getting through the gate without Nelly to hold the sheep back, but she managed it.

"What's going on now?" said Pink 38 huffily.

"And where's Old Smelly?" asked Yellow 14.

"I think the farmer's going to try to round us up on her own!" laughed Pink 38, with a cheeky glint in her eye.

"Oh, this is going to be fun!" grinned Yellow 14 mischievously.

But then Nan picked up the sack of sheep food.

"Wait a minute, she's got food in that sack! FOOD!" cried Pink 38 excitedly, and promptly raced over to Nan.

"FOOD? THERE'S FOOD?" bleated Yellow 14, and charged after her.

"FOOOOOOOOOD!" cried the rest of the flock greedily, and they all belted over towards Nan.

"NOOOO!" yelled Nan. "STOP! You'll knock me over."

But the sheep kept going. Nan tried to jump out of the way, but Pink 38 shot between her legs. The sheep's thick woolly fleece caught on Nan's overalls and lifted her right off her feet. Poor old Nan found herself sitting astride Pink 38 and riding her – backwards!

"Put me down, you ridiculous wobbly wool bag!" yelled Nan. She dropped the sack of food and clung on to Pink 38's fleece with both hands. When it hit the ground, the paper sack burst open and sheep food scattered all over the grass. Pink 38 darted around to get some, and Nan slithered off sideways.

Nelly was snoring softly when suddenly the kitchen door burst open and Nan stormed in.

"Those silly sheep are the absolute limit!" she cried, kicking off her wellies and plonking herself down at the table.

Nelly went over and put her head on Nan's knee.

"It's no good," said Nan, scratching Nelly's ears. "We're getting too old for this malarkey."

"Huh! Speak for yourself," Nelly thought.

"Enough is enough! Something will have to be done," announced Nan firmly.

Chapter 6
Special Speedy
Delivery

Thursday

The following morning, Nelly felt much better. Nan, on the other hand, didn't seem herself at all.

For a start, she got up very late. When she finally sloped into the kitchen, she was still in her pyjamas and yawning her head off.

"Good morning, Nelly," she said, ruffling the sheepdog's ears.

"Huh! More like 'good afternoon'," thought Nelly.

"Sorry, old girl. You must be hungry," said Nan, giving the sheepdog her breakfast.

"Hungry? I'm starving!" thought Nelly, wolfing it down.

"Slumbering shepherds! I haven't had a lie-in for fifty years!" said Nan, stretching. "I think I'll treat myself to a cooked breakfast," she added. She got out the frying pan, whistling loudly. Nelly was astonished.

"That's odd," thought Nelly. "Why aren't we going out to the field?"

After breakfast, Nan got dressed, but they still didn't go outside. Nan just sat at the table looking up stuff on her laptop – for *ages*. Nelly was desperate to go outside. She scratched at the door. Nan let her out.

When Nelly came back in, Nan was on the phone.

"And you'll deliver it this afternoon?" she was saying. "Fantastic."

"What's going on?" thought the sheepdog anxiously.

She soon found out!

In the afternoon, a large lorry pulled into the farmyard.

Nelly shot outside. "Who are you? What are you doing?" she barked furiously.

"It's all right, Nelly," laughed Nan, coming out into the farmyard.

"I'll be the judge of that!" growled Nelly, still on guard.

Two men climbed out of the truck, and lowered the rear door like a ramp.

"Sign here, please," said one of the men, holding out a pad to Nan.

"I can't wait to have a go on it!" she cried excitedly, as she signed. She was like a little toddler getting a new toy.

"A go on what?" thought Nelly suspiciously.

The other man put on a crash helmet and leaped inside the truck.

VROOOOOM! VROOOOM!

He roared down the ramp on a huge and powerful quad bike! He stopped the bike right in front of Nan, revving the engine furiously and showing off.

VROOM-
VROOM-
VROOM!

"My go!" yelled Nan over the noise.

"Oh, for crying out loud! She's not going to try and ride that thing, is she?" thought Nelly. "I can't look."

But Nan was. One of the men handed Nan a crash helmet and gave her a quick lesson on how to ride the quad bike. Then she took off around the farmyard.

"Yahoo!" whooped Nan.

"Wow! Look at her go," said one of the men. "She's super speedy!"

"It's a doddle," yelled Nan, whizzing around the farmyard. "It's just like riding a motorbike – only easier."

"Well, she's definitely not getting me on that!" thought Nelly in horror.

Both men shook their heads and roared with laughter. Then they shut the lorry door and drove away.

"Come on, Nelly," called Nan. "Let's go and visit the sheep. Up you get." She patted the space next to her on the quad bike.

"You have got to be kidding me!" thought Nelly, backing away.

"Don't be such a wimp!" scoffed Nan. "It's brilliant fun."

"Wimp? Nobody calls me a wimp," thought Nelly. She jumped on to the quad bike and sat next to Nan. "Well, it's a lot easier than scrambling up on to old Rusty Guts," she thought.

Nan revved the engine. "Hold tight!" she cried, and they zoomed out of the yard and along the lane up to the sheep field.

"Woo-hoo!" hollered Nan.

Nelly grinned happily with her tongue lolling out. "This is brilliant!" she barked. Nan drove the quad bike into the field. The sheep hung back uneasily.

"What on earth is that?" demanded Pink 38, pricking up her ears in surprise.

"I don't know, but whatever it is, I don't like the look of it," replied Yellow 14. They stamped their front feet crossly.

"Let's see if those loopy old wool bags can outrun me now!" chuckled Nan.
VROOOOOOM!

Nan roared across the field around one side, and Nelly shot off around the other. They ran rings around the sheep!

"BAA! BAAA! BAAAAA!" bleated the horrified sheep.

"Oi, that's not fair!" complained Pink 38.

"That's cheating!" bleated Yellow 14.

"Who says?" laughed Nelly.

"Walloping welly boots! Those nightmare naughty sheep are no match for us now!" yelled Nan. Then she stopped and looked at the sheep sternly. "Tomorrow, you lot are coming in for shearing," she told them firmly.

"And no mucking about," added Nelly.

But things didn't go quite the way they planned.

Chapter 7
Rustlers!

Much later, in the middle of the night, Nelly was fast asleep and snoring. She was having a lovely dream about herding a bunch of beautifully well-behaved sheep into pens. But suddenly she woke with a start.

She could hear sheep bleating. *Real* sheep bleating. It was *her* sheep bleating!

"What's going on out there?" she barked furiously.

Two minutes later, there was a loud
VROOOM!

Nan and Nelly roared up the lane to
the field on the quad bike. When they
got there, the gate was wide open and
a lorry was parked in the middle of the
field. The sheep had been rounded up in
the pen Nan had made, and two people
were herding them on to the lorry!

"Festering foot rot!" cried Nan. "They're stealing my sheep!" She snatched up her phone and called the police. Then she tore across the field on the quad bike, headlamps blazing.

"Put those sheep back!" barked Nelly furiously by Nan's side.

"It's the farmer!" cried the thieves. But by now they'd loaded the flock into the lorry. So they jumped into the cab and drove off, through the open gateway and down the lane.

"Shuddering sheep stealers! STOP!" bellowed Nan, tearing along behind them down the narrow lane and flashing her lights furiously. "You won't get away with this!"

As a matter of fact, the thieves didn't get away at all. Because suddenly, there was a SCREECH!

A police car zoomed up the lane, coming the other way. The truck was trapped between the police and the quad bike. The sheep rustlers leaped out of the cab, jumped over the fence and ran off across the field.

"Come back here!" yelled Nan.

Nelly shot off after them. Nan and the police officers followed as fast as they could. By the time they'd caught up with Nelly, she had rounded the thieves up and was circling around them, snarling menacingly.

"How dare you take my sheep," she growled.

"Call it off!" begged one of the thieves.

"Nice doggy," said the other one anxiously.

"Rumbling rustlers! Well done, Nelly!" cried Nan.

"We're arresting you for trying to steal sheep," said the police, leading the thieves off to their police car.

"Hang on a minute," said Nan. "What about my sheep? They're all stuck in the lorry."

"Do you want them put back in the field?" asked the police.

Nan thought for a second, and then grinned. "No, I'd like them put in the barn."

So the police made the thieves drive the lorry down to the farmyard and unload the sheep into the barn.

"BAA! BAA! BAAAA!" cried the confused sheep as they followed Pink 38 out of the darkness of the lorry and into the brightly lit barn.

"What's going on now?" cried Pink 38 stroppily.

"How did we get here?" bleated Yellow 14, looking around in surprise.

"In the back of a lorry," replied Nelly dryly. "Where did you think it was taking you?"

"How should I know?" replied Yellow 14. "They didn't say."

"Nobody bothers to tell us anything," huffed Pink 38.

Nelly was frankly amazed at the stupidity of the sheep. "Let me get this straight," she said. "You happily walked into the back of a strange lorry, herded in by a couple of complete strangers, and in the middle of the night? Why? Why would you do that?"

"Um ... er ... they had sheep food." Pink 38 blushed sheepishly.

"Oh, good grief," groaned Nelly, rolling her eyes.

Nan thanked the police for their help, and then she went back into the barn.

"At last," she sighed contentedly, as she looked at the sea of sheep milling around. "Finally those silly old fleece-bags are safely in the barn and ready for shearing. Fluttering fleeces, what a week!"

About the author

You're not going to believe this, but
I used to have a sheep farm – and we
milked the sheep. Honestly! We had
about one hundred and fifty sheep, and
most of them were stroppy like Pink
38! But we didn't need a sheepdog. Our
greedy sheep ran to us if we just rattled a
bucket of food! My favourite sheep was
called Alice.